From Seed to Pumpkin

By Jan Kottke

Welcome Books

Children's Press
A Division of Grolier Publishing
New York / London / Hong Kong / Sydney
Danbury, Connecticut

Photo Credits: Cover and all photos © Dwight Kuhn
Contributing Editors: Mark Beyer and Eliza Berkowitz
Book Design: MaryJane Wojciechowski

Visit Children's Press on the Internet at:
http://publishing.grolier.com

Library of Congress Cataloging-in-Publication Data

Kottke, Jan.
  From seed to pumpkin / by Jan Kottke.
    p. cm. — (How things grow)
  Includes bibliographical references and index.
  Summary: Illustrations and simple text describe how a pumpkin seed grows into a plant
that produces pumpkins.
  ISBN 0-516-23309-2 (lib. bdg.) — ISBN 0-516-23509-5 (pbk.)
  1. Pumpkin—Juvenile literature. [1. Pumpkin.] I. Title.
SB347.K68 2000
635'.62—dc21

                                                                    00-024367

Contents

This is a pumpkin **seed** sitting in **soil**.

A **shoot** is growing from the pumpkin seed.

The shoot grows into the ground.

5

A **stem** grows from the seed.

It has two leaves.

The pumpkin seed is now a plant.

It has many leaves.

It also has a flower.

9

The pumpkin flower will help a pumpkin to grow.

The **pollen** inside the flower will help to make more pumpkins.

A bee takes pollen from the flower.

The bee brings the pollen to other flowers.

13

The pumpkin flower is changing.

The **petals** are getting smaller.

It doesn't look like a flower anymore.

15

The pumpkin flower is almost gone.

The bottom of the flower is getting bigger.

It is becoming a pumpkin.

Pumpkins grow in a **patch**.

These pumpkins are growing larger.

They are almost ready to pick.

19

Pumpkins are picked when they are **ripe**.

Ripe pumpkins are big and orange.

New Words

patch (**patch**) a place where something grows

petals (**peh**-tuhlz) parts of a flower

pollen (**pah**-len) a powder that helps flowers make seeds

ripe (**reyep**) fully grown and ready to pick

seed (**seed**) the part of a plant that makes a new plant

shoot (**shoot**) the part of a plant that grows into the ground

soil (**soyl**) dirt

stem (**stem**) thin part of a plant that grows from the ground

To Find Out More

Books

Big Pumpkin
by Erica Silverman
Simon & Schuster Children's

Pumpkin Pumpkin
by Jeanne Titherington
William Morrow & Company

I'm a Seed
by Jean Marzollo
Scholastic

The Pumpkin Patch
by Elizabeth King
Dutton Children's Books

Web Sites

Pumpkins & More
http://www.urbanext.uiuc.edu/pumpkins/index.html
This site has pumpkin cooking recipes, growing tips, and fun facts. It also has links to fun pumpkin activities.

The Giant Pumpkin Web Site
http://www.giantpumpkins.com
Includes tips on growing pumpkins, pictures of giant pumpkins, and links to other sites. It also contains a video to watch.

Index

About the Author

Jan Kottke is the owner/director of several preschools in the Tidewater area of Virginia. A lifelong early education professional, she is completing a phonics reading series for preschoolers.

Reading Consultants

Kris Flynn, Coordinator, Small School District Literacy, The San Diego County Office of Education

Shelly Forys, Certified Reading Recovery Specialist, W.J. Zahnow Elementary School, Waterloo, IL

Peggy McNamara, Professor, Bank Street College of Education, Reading and Literacy Program